FOREWORD

The PUPIL should read carefully the teacher's assignment. Then check in the column for the day and practice as instructed. In this way everything practiced will be recorded daily.

The TEACHER should mark at the time of the lesson the standard of the pupil's work for each subject as follows:
"A" excellent,   "B" good,   "C" average,   "D" below average,
"E" unsatisfactory.

The PARENT should sign the weekly record after the lesson, thus following more closely the pupil's progress.

PRACTICE RECORD

For week beginning..*(date)*

TEACHER'S ASSIGNMENT AND INSTRUCTIONS	PUPIL'S DAILY RECORD						TEACHER'S RATING
	Mon.	Tues.	Wed.	Thur.	Fri.	Sat.	
TECHNICAL EXERCISES..................							
SCALES..................							
CHORDS..................							
ARPEGGIOS..................							
STUDIES..................							
SIGHT-READING..................							
EAR TRAINING..................							
PIECES..................							
....							
....							
MISCELLANEOUS..................							
....							

Remarks to the parents...

Parent's Signature...

Date...

NOTES

PRACTICE RECORD

For week beginning..*(date)*

TEACHER'S ASSIGNMENT AND INSTRUCTIONS	PUPIL'S DAILY RECORD						TEACHER RATING
	Mon.	Tues.	Wed.	Thur.	Fri.	Sat.	
TECHNICAL EXERCISES..							
SCALES..							
CHORDS...							
ARPEGGIOS...							
STUDIES...							
SIGHT-READING..							
EAR TRAINING...							
PIECES...							
....							
....							
MISCELLANEOUS..							
....							

Remarks to the parents...

Parent's Signature...

Date...

NOTES

PRACTICE RECORD

For week beginning .... *(date)*

TEACHER'S ASSIGNMENT AND INSTRUCTIONS	PUPIL'S DAILY RECORD						TEACHER'S RATING
	Mon.	Tues.	Wed.	Thur.	Fri.	Sat.	
TECHNICAL EXERCISES...							
SCALES...							
CHORDS..							
ARPEGGIOS..							
STUDIES...							
SIGHT-READING..							
EAR TRAINING..							
PIECES...							
....							
....							
MISCELLANEOUS..							
....							

Remarks to the parents...

Parent's Signature...

Date...

NOTES

PRACTICE RECORD

For week beginning...*(date)*

TEACHER'S ASSIGNMENT AND INSTRUCTIONS	PUPIL'S DAILY RECORD						TEACHER RATING
	Mon.	Tues.	Wed.	Thur.	Fri.	Sat.	
TECHNICAL EXERCISES.............							
SCALES................................							
CHORDS...............................							
ARPEGGIOS...........................							
STUDIES...............................							
SIGHT-READING......................							
EAR TRAINING.......................							
PIECES................................							
....							
....							
MISCELLANEOUS.....................							
....							

Remarks to the parents..

Parent's Signature..

Date...

NOTES

PRACTICE RECORD

For week beginning..(date)

TEACHER'S ASSIGNMENT AND INSTRUCTIONS	PUPIL'S DAILY RECORD						TEACHER RATING
	Mon.	Tues.	Wed.	Thur.	Fri.	Sat.	
TECHNICAL EXERCISES..							
SCALES...							
CHORDS..							
ARPEGGIOS..							
STUDIES...							
SIGHT-READING.......................................							
EAR TRAINING..							
PIECES..							
....							
....							
MISCELLANEOUS......................................							
....							

Remarks to the parents..

Parent's Signature..

Date..

NOTES

PRACTICE RECORD

For week beginning..*(date)*

TEACHER'S ASSIGNMENT AND INSTRUCTIONS	PUPIL'S DAILY RECORD						TEACHER RATING
	Mon.	Tues.	Wed.	Thur.	Fri.	Sat.	
TECHNICAL EXERCISES...							....
SCALES..							....
CHORDS..							....
ARPEGGIOS..							....
STUDIES..							....
SIGHT-READING..							....
EAR TRAINING...							....
PIECES...							....
....							....
....							....
MISCELLANEOUS..							....
....							....

Remarks to the parents...

Parent's Signature...

Date...

NOTES

PRACTICE RECORD

For week beginning..*(date)*

TEACHER'S ASSIGNMENT AND INSTRUCTIONS	PUPIL'S DAILY RECORD						TEACHER RATING
	Mon.	Tues.	Wed.	Thur.	Fri.	Sat.	
TECHNICAL EXERCISES..........							
SCALES..........							
CHORDS..........							
ARPEGGIOS..........							
STUDIES..........							
SIGHT-READING..........							
EAR TRAINING..........							
PIECES..........							
....							
....							
MISCELLANEOUS..........							
....							

Remarks to the parents..

Parent's Signature..

Date..

NOTES

PRACTICE RECORD

For week beginning..*(date)*

TEACHER'S ASSIGNMENT AND INSTRUCTIONS	PUPIL'S DAILY RECORD						TEACHER'S RATING
	Mon.	Tues.	Wed.	Thur.	Fri.	Sat.	
TECHNICAL EXERCISES..........							
SCALES..........							
CHORDS..........							
ARPEGGIOS..........							
STUDIES..........							
SIGHT-READING..........							
EAR TRAINING..........							
PIECES..........							
....							
....							
MISCELLANEOUS..........							
....							

Remarks to the parents...

Parent's Signature...

Date...

NOTES

PRACTICE RECORD

For week beginning..*(date)*

TEACHER'S ASSIGNMENT AND INSTRUCTIONS	PUPIL'S DAILY RECORD						TEACHER RATING
	Mon.	Tues.	Wed.	Thur.	Fri.	Sat.	
TECHNICAL EXERCISES...........................							
SCALES...........................							
CHORDS...........................							
ARPEGGIOS...........................							
STUDIES...........................							
SIGHT-READING...........................							
EAR TRAINING...........................							
PIECES...........................							
....							
....							
MISCELLANEOUS...........................							
....							

Remarks to the parents..

Parent's Signature..

Date..

NOTES

PRACTICE RECORD

For week beginning...*(date)*

TEACHER'S ASSIGNMENT AND INSTRUCTIONS	PUPIL'S DAILY RECORD						TEACHER RATING
	Mon.	Tues.	Wed.	Thur.	Fri.	Sat.	
TECHNICAL EXERCISES..................................							
SCALES...							
CHORDS..							
ARPEGGIOS...							
STUDIES...							
SIGHT-READING.......................................							
EAR TRAINING...							
PIECES...							
....							
....							
MISCELLANEOUS......................................							
....							

Remarks to the parents...

Parent's Signature...

Date...

NOTES

PRACTICE RECORD

For week beginning..*(date)*

TEACHER'S ASSIGNMENT AND INSTRUCTIONS	PUPIL'S DAILY RECORD						TEACHER'S RATING
	Mon.	Tues.	Wed.	Thur.	Fri.	Sat.	
TECHNICAL EXERCISES.................................							....
SCALES..							
CHORDS...							
ARPEGGIOS..							
STUDIES...							
SIGHT-READING.....................................							
EAR TRAINING......................................							
PIECES..							
....							
....							
MISCELLANEOUS....................................							
....							

Remarks to the parents...

Parent's Signature..

Date..

NOTES

PRACTICE RECORD

For week beginning .... *(date)*

TEACHER'S ASSIGNMENT AND INSTRUCTIONS	PUPIL'S DAILY RECORD						TEACHE RATINC
	Mon.	Tues.	Wed.	Thur.	Fri.	Sat.	
TECHNICAL EXERCISES..							
SCALES..							
CHORDS..							
ARPEGGIOS..							
STUDIES..							
SIGHT-READING..							
EAR TRAINING..							
PIECES..							
....							
....							
MISCELLANEOUS..							
....							

Remarks to the parents...

Parent's Signature...

Date...

NOTES

PRACTICE RECORD

For week beginning .... *(date)*

TEACHER'S ASSIGNMENT AND INSTRUCTIONS	PUPIL'S DAILY RECORD						TEACHER'S RATING
	Mon.	Tues.	Wed.	Thur.	Fri.	Sat.	
TECHNICAL EXERCISES..........................							....
SCALES..							....
CHORDS...							....
ARPEGGIOS...							....
STUDIES...							....
SIGHT-READING...................................							....
EAR TRAINING.....................................							....
PIECES...							....
....							....
....							....
MISCELLANEOUS...................................							....
....							....

Remarks to the parents...

Parent's Signature...

Date..

NOTES

PRACTICE RECORD

For week beginning..*(date)*

TEACHER'S ASSIGNMENT AND INSTRUCTIONS	PUPIL'S DAILY RECORD						TEACHER RATING
	Mon.	Tues.	Wed.	Thur.	Fri.	Sat.	
TECHNICAL EXERCISES..							....
SCALES..							
CHORDS...							
ARPEGGIOS...							
STUDIES..							
SIGHT-READING..							
EAR TRAINING...							
PIECES..							
....							
....							
MISCELLANEOUS...							
....							

Remarks to the parents..

Parent's Signature...

Date...

NOTES

PRACTICE RECORD

For week beginning..*(date)*

TEACHER'S ASSIGNMENT AND INSTRUCTIONS	PUPIL'S DAILY RECORD						TEACHER RATING
	Mon.	Tues.	Wed.	Thur.	Fri.	Sat.	
TECHNICAL EXERCISES....................							....
SCALES.................................							....
CHORDS.................................							....
ARPEGGIOS..............................							....
STUDIES................................							....
SIGHT-READING.........................							....
EAR TRAINING..........................							....
PIECES.................................							....
....							....
....							....
MISCELLANEOUS.........................							....
....							....

Remarks to the parents..

Parent's Signature..

Date..

NOTES

PRACTICE RECORD

For week beginning..*(date)*

TEACHER'S ASSIGNMENT AND INSTRUCTIONS	PUPIL'S DAILY RECORD						TEACHER RATING
	Mon.	Tues.	Wed.	Thur.	Fri.	Sat.	
TECHNICAL EXERCISES....................							
SCALES....................							
CHORDS....................							
ARPEGGIOS....................							
STUDIES....................							
SIGHT-READING....................							
EAR TRAINING....................							
PIECES....................							
....							
....							
MISCELLANEOUS....................							
....							

Remarks to the parents..

Parent's Signature..

Date..

NOTES

PRACTICE RECORD

For week beginning..*(date)*

TEACHER'S ASSIGNMENT AND INSTRUCTIONS	PUPIL'S DAILY RECORD						TEACHER RATING
	Mon.	Tues.	Wed.	Thur.	Fri.	Sat.	
TECHNICAL EXERCISES...........................							
SCALES..							
CHORDS..							
ARPEGGIOS.....................................							
STUDIES.......................................							
SIGHT-READING.................................							
EAR TRAINING..................................							
PIECES..							
....							
....							
MISCELLANEOUS.................................							
....							

Remarks to the parents..

Parent's Signature..

Date..

NOTES

PRACTICE RECORD

For week beginning..*(date)*

TEACHER'S ASSIGNMENT AND INSTRUCTIONS	PUPIL'S DAILY RECORD						TEACHER RATING
	Mon.	Tues.	Wed.	Thur.	Fri.	Sat.	
TECHNICAL EXERCISES..........							
SCALES..........							
CHORDS..........							
ARPEGGIOS..........							
STUDIES..........							
SIGHT-READING..........							
EAR TRAINING..........							
PIECES..........							
....							
....							
MISCELLANEOUS..........							
....							

Remarks to the parents..

Parent's Signature..

Date..

NOTES

PRACTICE RECORD

For week beginning .... *(date)*

TEACHER'S ASSIGNMENT AND INSTRUCTIONS	PUPIL'S DAILY RECORD						TEACHER RATING
	Mon.	Tues.	Wed.	Thur.	Fri.	Sat.	
TECHNICAL EXERCISES...							
SCALES..							
CHORDS..							
ARPEGGIOS...							
STUDIES...							
SIGHT-READING..							
EAR TRAINING...							
PIECES...							
....							
....							
MISCELLANEOUS..							
....							

Remarks to the parents...

Parent's Signature...

Date...

NOTES

PRACTICE RECORD

For week beginning..*(date)*

TEACHER'S ASSIGNMENT AND INSTRUCTIONS	PUPIL'S DAILY RECORD						TEACHER RATING
	Mon.	Tues.	Wed.	Thur.	Fri.	Sat.	
TECHNICAL EXERCISES...							....
SCALES..							....
CHORDS...							....
ARPEGGIOS...							....
STUDIES...							....
SIGHT-READING..							....
EAR TRAINING..							....
PIECES..							....
....							....
....							....
MISCELLANEOUS..							....
....							....

Remarks to the parents...

Parent's Signature...

Date..

NOTES

Guide to Sight-Playing

Based on sight-playing tests of Examination requirements.

- Before playing at sight look at the music and observe essential details such as the clefs, key-signature, time-values of notes, and so on.

- Prepare your fingers placing them over their correct keys (particularly in the lower grades where a five-finger position is used) and try to play looking at the music and not the hands or the keys (keyboard).

- Play steadily and without hurry, and preserve the same tempo to the end of the piece. Do not stop or go back to correct mistakes. Keep going to maintain the rhythmic flow of the music.

- Always try to read a beat or more ahead of what you are playing.

A good sight reader should be familiar with:

1—notes on the lines and the spaces in the treble and bass clefs, including leger lines.

2—notes moving by steps scalewise, like

3—notes separated by intervals, such as

4—chords in various keys and positions

5—various ornaments (embellishments), such as

6—time values and rhythmical groupings such as

7—phrasing and expression marks, tempo indication etc.

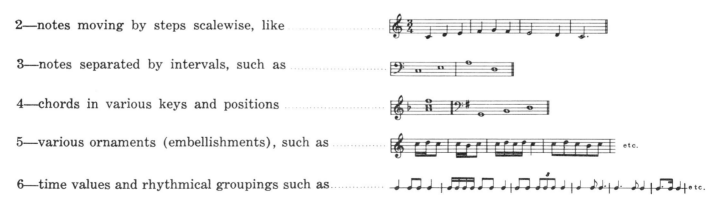

Guide to Ear-Training

Based on the ear-tests of Examination requirements

1—Sing or hum familiar tunes (songs).

2—Sing the three notes of a major or minor triad varying the order of the notes.

3—Sing the notes of major and minor scales as well as of broken chords while playing them on the piano.

4—Sing or hum various intervals. This may be helped by the use of sol-fa syllables or numbers, i.e. "doh, ray" (1-2), "doh, me" (1-3) "doh, fah" (1-4), "doh, soh" (1-5), and so on.
  You may also associate intervals with the beginning of well-known melodies such as: "Old Black Joe" (+3), "O, Canada" (–3), "British Grenadiers" (per. 4th), "Baa-baa, Black Sheep" (per. 5th), "My Bonnie Lies Over The Ocean" (+6), for intervals **above** a given note, and "Good Night Ladies" (+3), "O Come All Ye Faithful" (per. 4th), "Bach's Minuet in G" (per. 5th), for intervals **below** a given note.

5—To imitate a tune previously played by the teacher or the examiner, sing the tune (mentally) first, and make sure you have the first note right.

6—To recognize (distinguish) a chord played by the teacher or the examiner, decide whether it is major, or minor (or dominant or diminished seventh) first; then, the BASS note is what matters.
  For the RHYTHMICAL part of the ear-test:
  (a) Clap or tap the rhythm of familiar tunes, or of tunes played by the teacher.
  (b) Point to the rhythms played by the teacher and repeat the rhythm while reading the example such as:

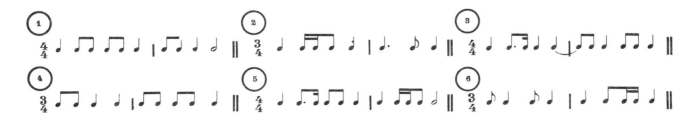

FINGERING of SCALES and CHORDS

The most commonly used fingering in scales beginning on a *white* key is: ⌐1 2 3⌐ ⌐1 2 3 4⌐ repeating the *two groups of fingering* when playing more than one octave, and ending the scale with the 5th finger — in *all scales beginning on a white key*, (except F scale in the right hand) — the right hand ascending, left hand descending.

Thus the 4th finger of the right hand plays the seventh note (leading note, or te); the 4th finger of the left hand — the second note (supertonic, re).

In scales beginning on a *black* key, the *THUMB* plays the *first white key* ascending in the RIGHT HAND, descending in the LEFT HAND. The rest of the fingers will follow in the two groups ⌐1 2 3⌐ ⌐1 2 3 4⌐

Thus the RIGHT HAND will have the thumb on F and C; the 4th finger on B♭ in *all "flat" scales*; — the thumb on E and B; the 4th finger on A♯ in *all "sharp" scales*.

TRIADS: 1 ② 5 in the second inversion right hand, first inversion left hand; 1 3 5 in all other positions.

TABLE of SCALES with CADENCES

The Chromatic Scale

FINGERING of ARPEGGIOS

The *thumb* plays the *first white key* ascending in the RIGHT HAND, descending in the LEFT HAND. All white keys begin with the thumb (or 5th finger) whether in root position or in an inversion.

Major Arpeggios

Dominant Seventh Chords

Diminished Seventh Chords

Student's Objective for Season 20____ -20____

PRACTICAL EXAMINATION: GRADE ....

THEORY EXAMINATION: GRADE ....

FESTIVAL WORK ....

....

REPERTOIRE ....

....

....

TECHNIQUE: EXERCISES ....

....

....

STUDIES ....

....

....

	SPEED		SPEED
SCALES	M.M. ♩ = ...	OCTAVES	M.M. ♩ = ...
CHORDS	M.M. ♩ = ...	DOUBLE THIRDS	M.M. ♩ = ...
ARPEGGIOS	M.M. ♩ = ...	HANON	M.M. ♩ = ...